COLOR-BY-NUMBERS MASTERPIECES

UNWIND AND RELEASE YOUR **CREATIVITY** BY BRINGING **ART** TO LIFE

This edition published by Parragon Books Ltd in 2016 and distributed by

Parragon Inc.
440 Park Avenue South, 13th Floor
New York, NY 10016
www.parragon.com

Images created by Lexi L'Esteve

ISBN 978-1-4748-3837-5
Printed in China

Bath • New York • Cologne • Melbourne • Delhi
Hong Kong • Shenzhen • Singapore

HOW TO USE THIS BOOK

Match the numbers with the colors to recreate some genuine works of art! Look at the numbers in the artwork and pair these up with the numbers in the color bar at the bottom of the image—this bar will guide you as to which colors to use in the different parts of the picture.

The images can be colored in with either colored pencils or felt tip pens. If you don't have a colored pencil or pen that is identical to the shade in the coloring bar then just pick a tone that is as close as possible. As long as the color is similar, it will not affect the overall look of the masterpiece so just work with what you have available.

The pictures in this book are arranged with all the portrait-shaped images first and are then followed by all the landscape-shaped images, so just turn the book around to start the landscape pictures. These color-by-numbers masterpieces are relaxing to complete and should take anything from 30 minutes to up to an hour to complete, but there is no restriction on how long you can spend on these. These color-by-numbers images will allow you to explore your creativity, particularly if you are not confident at drawing or sketching, so even a novice can recreate these beautiful works of art and unleash their imagination.

Once you've joined colored in all the images, you could remove each picture and frame the resulting image for a truly unique piece of art. The perforations along each page allow you to tear out any masterpiece, so you could give these to friends or display them around your own home.

The back pages of this book provides a small preview of each completed image, so be careful not to look at these in advance if you want to avoid a spoiler of the final results!

1	2	3	4	5	6	7	8	9	A	B	C	D

1           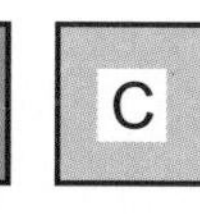   F

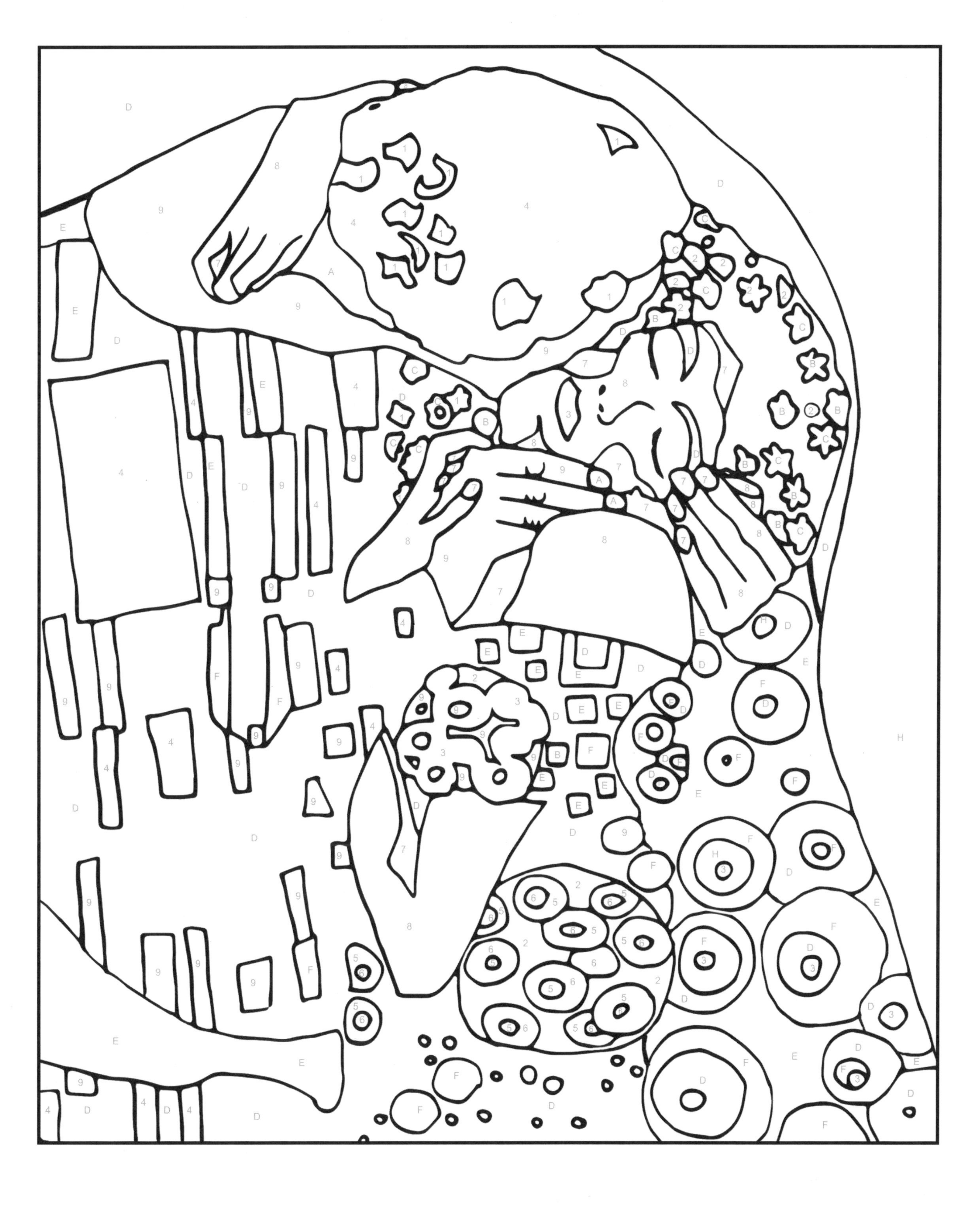

1 2 3 4 5 6 7 8 9 A B C D E F G H I

1 2 3 4 5 6 7 8 9 A B C D E F

1 2 3 4 5 6 7 8 9 A B C D E F G H I J

1
2
3
4
5
6
7
8
9
A
B
C
D
E
F
G
H
I

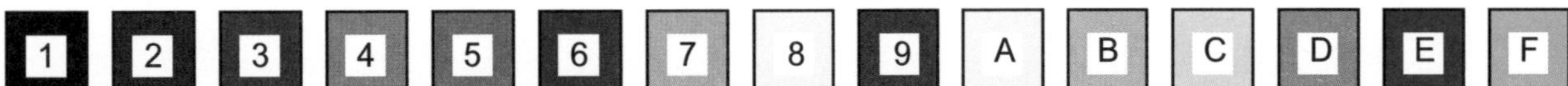
1 2 3 4 5 6 7 8 9 A B C D E F

1 2 3 4 5 6 7 8 9 A B C D E

1	2	3	4	5	6	7	8	9	A	B	C	D	E	F	G	H	I

1 2 3 4 5 6 7 8 9 A B C D E F G H I J K L M

1
2
3
4
5
6
7
8
9

1	2	3	4	5	6	7	8	9	A	B	C	D	E	F	G	H	I

1 2 3 4 5 6 7 8 9 A B C D E F G H I

1 2 3 4 5 6 7 8 9 A

1 2 3 4 5 6 7 8 9 A B C D E F G H I J K L

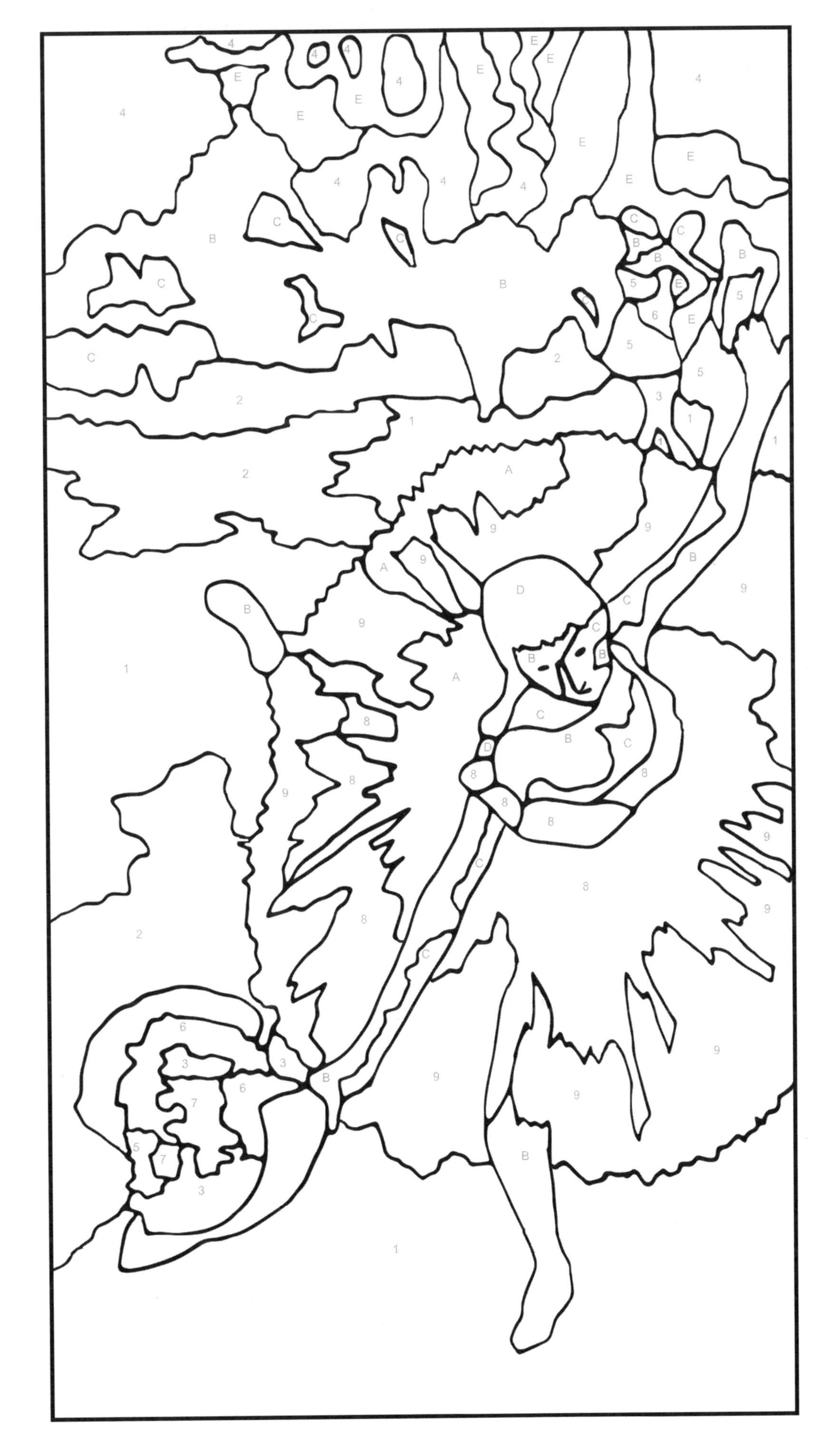

1 2  3 4  5 6 7 8 9 A B C D E

1
2
3
4
5
6
7
8
9
A
B
C
D
E
F
G
H
I

1
2
3
4
5
6
7
8
9
A
B

E

1 2 3 4 5 6 7 8 9 A B C D E

1
2
3
4
5
6
7
8
9
A
B

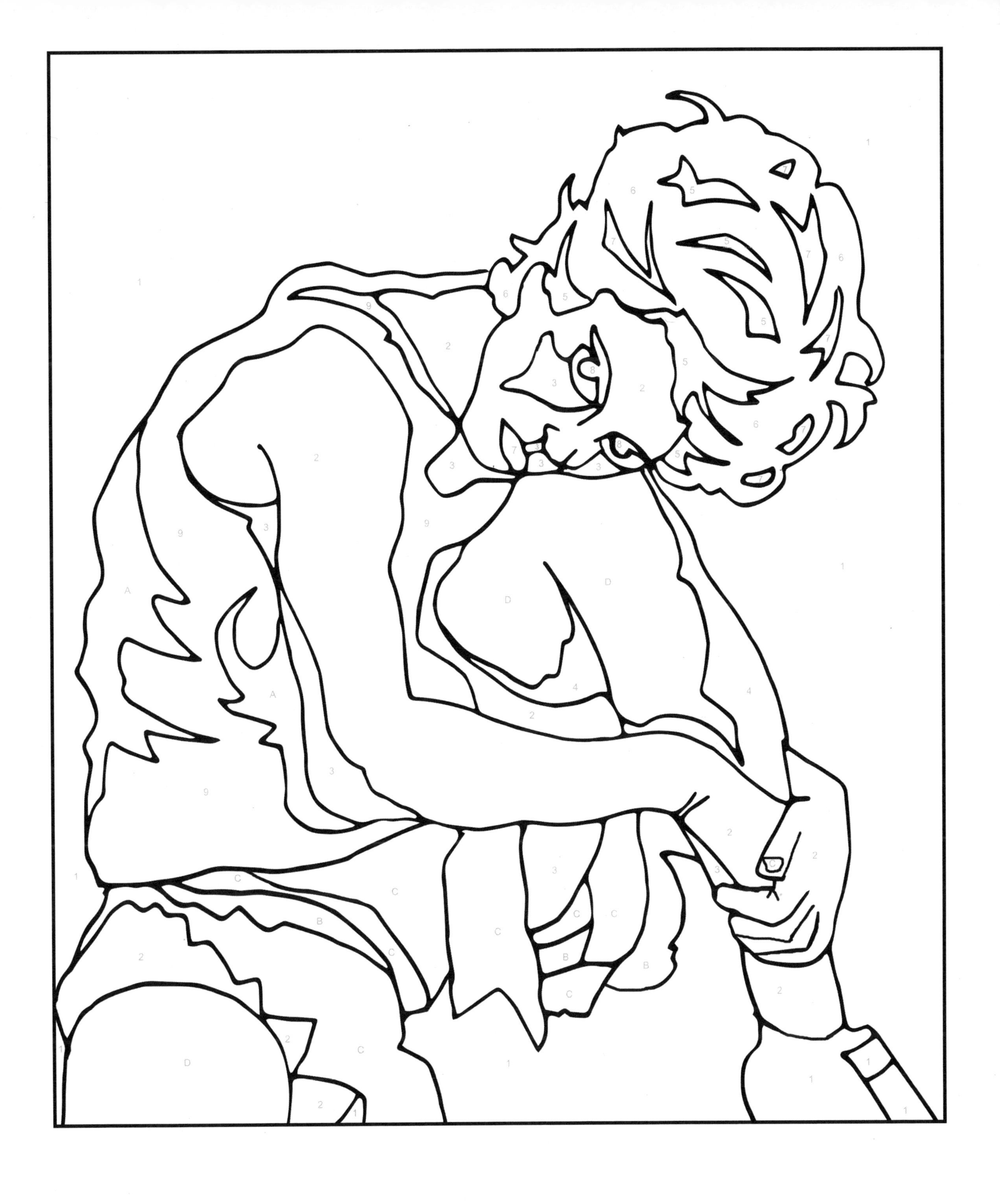

1 2 3 4 5 6 7 8 9 A B C D

1 2 3 4 5 6 7 8 9 A B C D E F

1 2 3 4 5 6 7 8 9

1 2 3 4 5 6 7 8 9 A B C D E

1 2 3 4 5 6 7 8 9 A B C D E F

1 2 3 4 5 6 7 8 9 A B C D E F G H I J K

1
2
3
4
5
6
7
8
9
A

1 2 3 4 5 6 7 8 9 A B C D E F G H I J K L

1
2
3
4
5
6
7
8
9
A
B
C
D
E
F
G
H

1	2	3	4	5	6	7	8	9	A	B	C	E	F	G	H	I

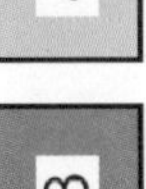

1 2 3 4 5 6 7 8 9 A B C D

1 2 3 4 5 6 7 8 9 A B C D E

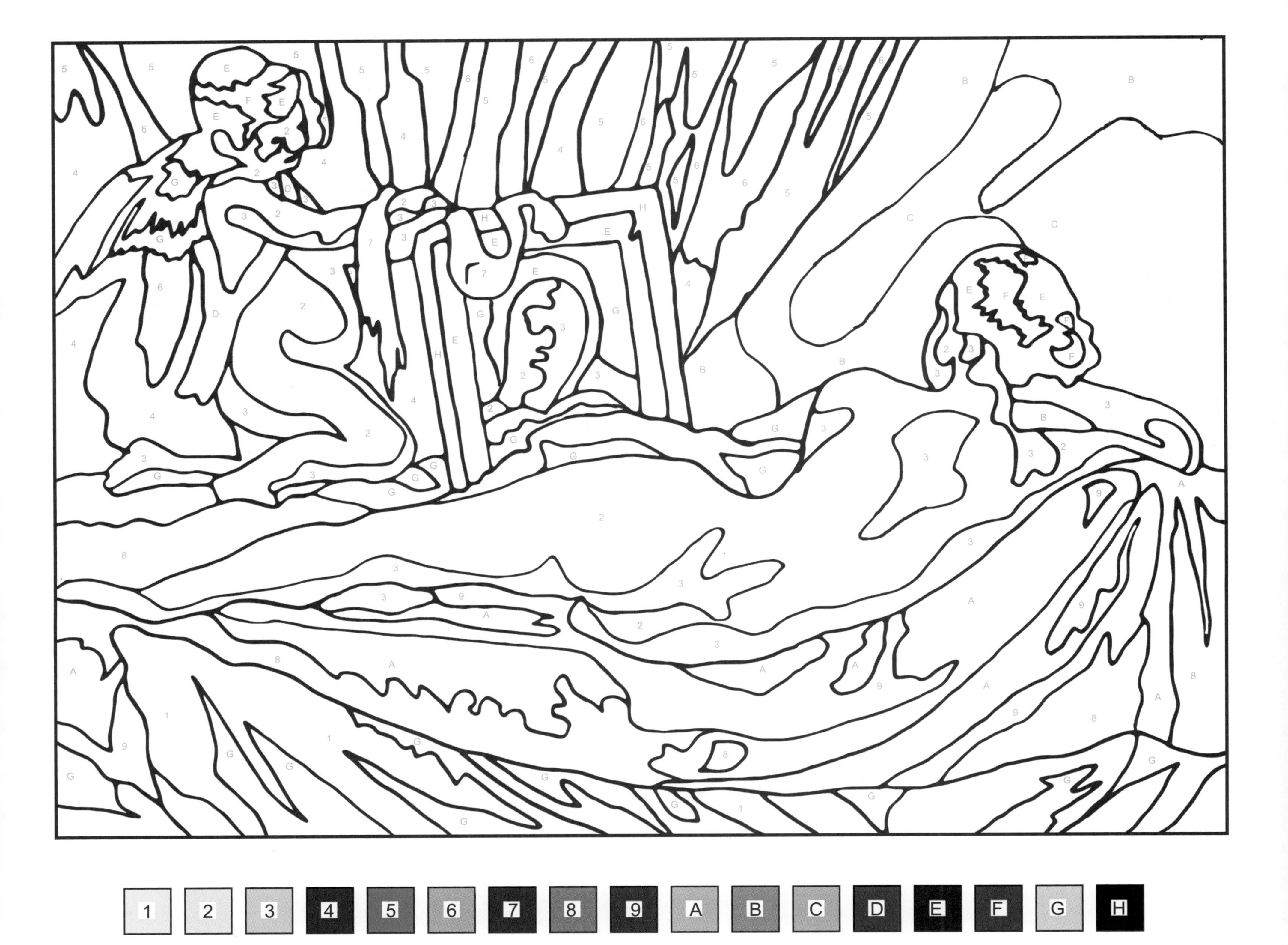
1 2 3 4 5 6 7 8 9 A B C D E F G H

1 2 3 4 5 6 7 8 9 A B C D E F G H I J K L M N O

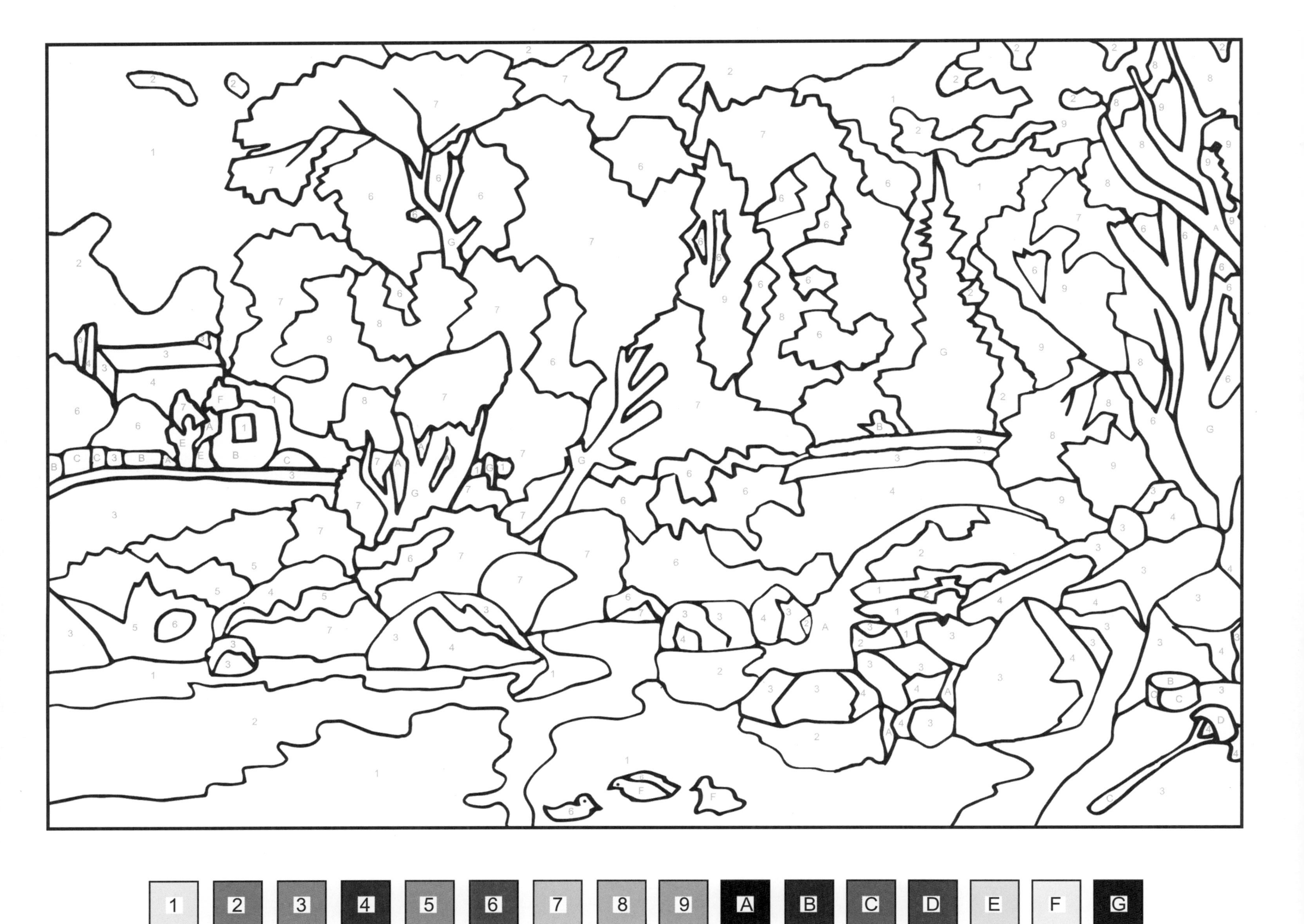
1
2
3
4
5
6
7
8
9
A
B
C
D
E
F
G

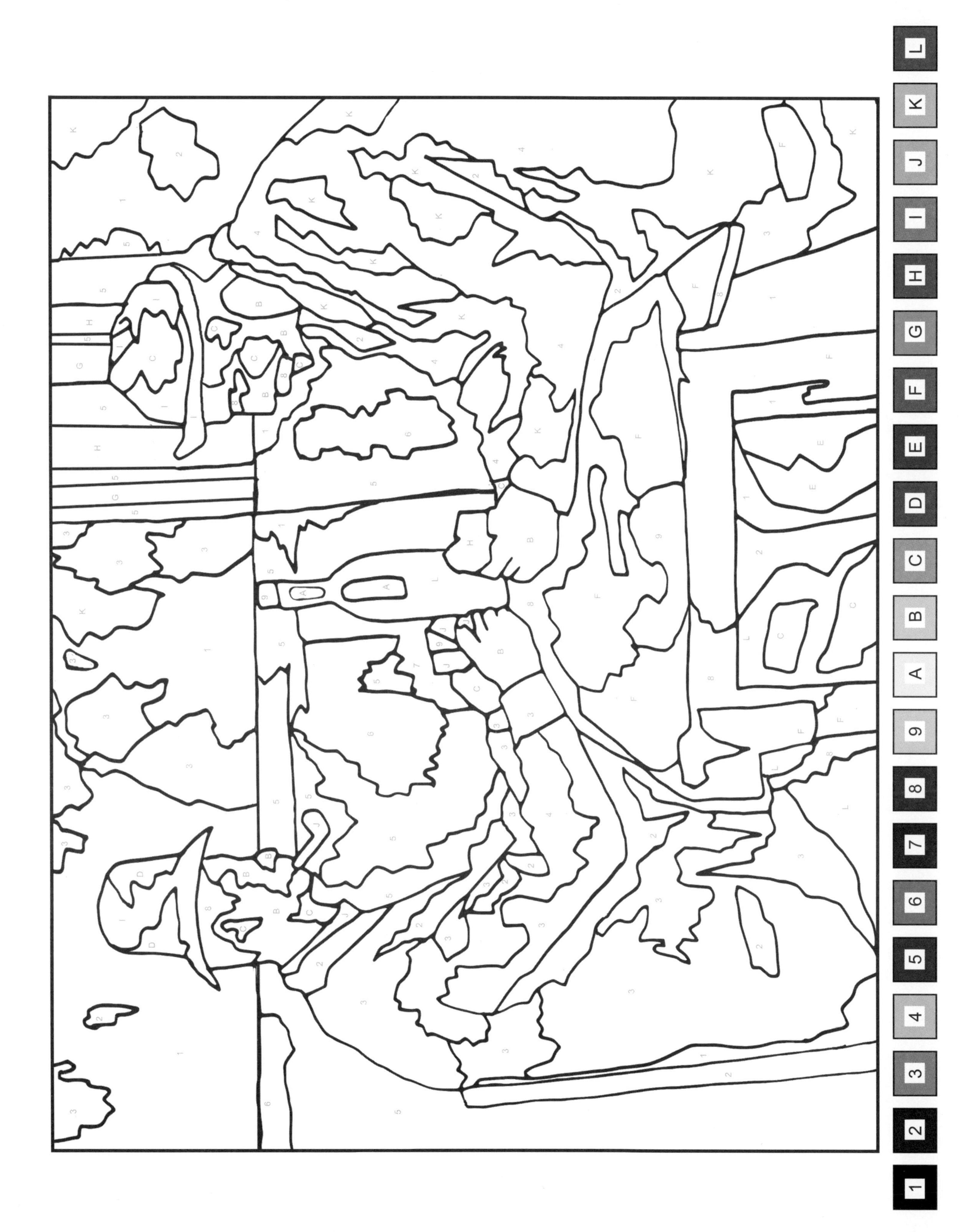

1 2 3 4 5 6 7 8 9 A B C D E F G H I J K

5. ***Self Portrait*** by Van Gogh

7. ***The Scream*** by Munch

1 2 3 4 5 6 7 8 9 A B C D E F G H I

9. ***The Kiss*** by Klimt

1 2 3 4 5 6 7 8 9 A B C D E F

11. ***Ophelia*** by Millais

1 2 3 4 5 6 7 8 9 A B C D E F G H I J

13. ***The Sistine Madonna*** by Raphael

15. ***Liberty Leading the People*** by Delacroix

17. ***The Balcony*** by Manet

19. ***Parham's Mill*** by Constable

21. ***Mäda Primavesi*** by Klimt

23. ***Bal du Moulin de la Galette*** by Renoir

25. ***Whistlejacket*** by Stubbs

27. ***At The Moulin Rouge, The Dance*** by Lautrec

29. ***Portrait of Henry VIII*** by Holbein the Younger

31. ***Portrait of Madame X*** by Singer Sargent

33. ***Beata Beatrix*** by Rossetti

35. ***Dancer with a Bouquet of Flowers*** by Degas

37. ***Portrait of Irene d'Anvers*** by Renoir

39. ***Portrait of a Man in a Red Turban*** by Van Eyck

1 2 3 4 5 6 7 8 9 A B C D E

41. ***The Laughing Cavalier*** by Hals

43. ***Portrait of a Young Woman*** by Botticelli

45. ***Self Portrait*** by Rembrandt

47. ***Seated Woman with Bent Knee*** by Schiele

49. ***The Arnolfini Portrait*** by Van Eyck

51. ***Sunflowers*** by Van Gogh

53. ***Mona Lisa*** by Da Vinci

1 2 3 4 5 6 7 8 9 A B C D E F

55. ***Girl with a Pearl Earring*** by Vermeer

1 2 3 4 5 6 7 8 9 A B C D E F G H I J K

57. ***American Gothic*** by Wood

1 2 3 4 5 6 7 8 9 A

59. ***The Great Wave*** by Hokusai

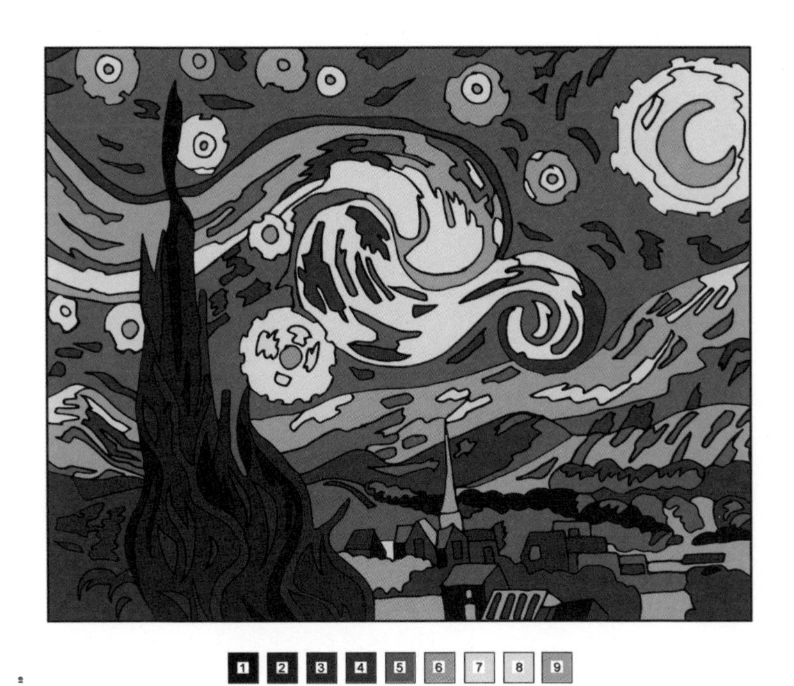

1 2 3 4 5 6 7 8 9

61. ***The Starry Night*** by Van Gogh

63. ***Whistler's Mother*** by Whistler

65. ***La Maja Vestida*** by Goya

67.***Parau Api*** by Gauguin

69. ***Traumgarten*** by Rousseau

1 2 3 4 5 6 7 8 9 A B C D

71. ***Leda and the Swan*** by Michelangelo

1 2 3 4 5 6 7 8 9 A B C D E

73. ***Water Lilies*** by Monet

1 2 3 4 5 6 7 8 9 A B C D E F G H I J K L M N O

75. ***Venus and Adonis*** by Rubens

1 2 3 4 5 6 7 8 9 A B C D E F G H

77. ***The Rokeby Venus*** by Velázquez

79. ***Bathers at Asnières*** by Seurat

81. ***Ivy Bridge*** by Turner

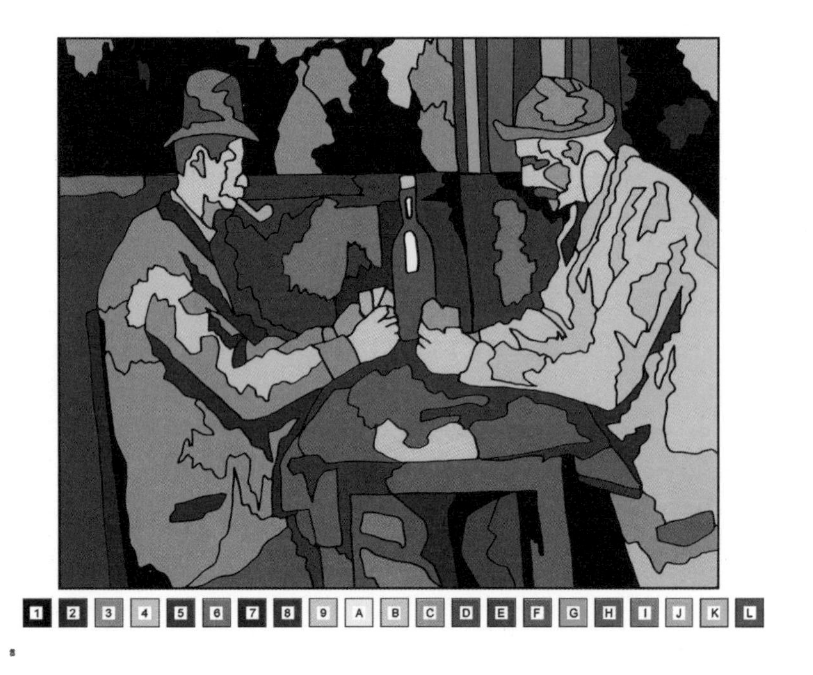

83. ***The Card Players*** by Cézanne

85. ***In the Conservatory*** by Manet